The Rainbow STACK

A Casual Guide to UX Design

JOSEPH S. JAWARA

Copyright © 2020 by Joseph S. Jawara.

All rights reserved. This book is protected by copyright. No part of this book may be reproduced or transmitted in any form or by any means, including as photocopies or scanned-in or other electronic copies, or utilized by any information storage and retrieval system without written permission from the copyright owner.

Printed in the United States of America.

Cover Design by 100Covers.com
Interior Design by FormattedBooks.com

CONTENTS

Introduction v

Part I: The Foundation

Hypotheses 1
Empathy 3
Define 7
Strategy 11
    Surveys 13
    Interviews 16
    User Personas 22

Part II: The Idea Factory

Ideate 31
Scope 39
Structure 43

Part III: The Build

Prototype 57
Skeleton 59
    Wireframing 61
    Labeling 63
Surface 69
Test 75
Conclusion 81
Bibliography 89

INTRODUCTION

"You become responsible forever for what you've tamed."

—Antoine de Saint-Exupéry

The process presented in this book is the direct result of trying to gain a deeper understanding of the entire user experience process. Through this journey, I became convinced that the techniques with which I was becoming familiar were solely results oriented. This meant that they could potentially exist in many different versions in many different places. While this was not a deal breaker, I found it difficult to rationalize my flow without a point of reference. I needed a single source of truth. I needed things to be laid out before me as a whole with their genesis indicated.

This book is many things but what it isn't, is a *how-to* manual. It won't show you the basics of design; it caters to the *why* instead of the *how*. This book is about *The Rainbow Stack*, the ability to build and execute every part of the design stack, from beginning to end, all by your lonesome. Though *The Rainbow Stack* can be used by anyone who wishes to more adequately fulfill their user needs, it is written with the following people in mind:

1. UX designers, who want to break free from their professional silos.
2. Design hopefuls, who are looking for a solid overview of the entire UX process.
3. Entrepreneurs, who want to make their product offering more compelling.

After we get through all the material and put the pieces of the user experience puzzle together, I think it will be pretty rewarding to see the final result.

Now it goes without saying that everything mentioned in this book, is subjective—that is, based on how I like to lay things out and make sense of them in my mind. My method may not be the best and it surely isn't the only one. With my disclaimer out of the way, let's jump right in.

Everything that we see around us has been designed; from the clothes on your back to the device you're probably reading these very words on. I know … very meta.

While I concede we won't be discussing the design of fashion accessories or physical products, we will be covering the process of creating digital products that delight their end users. That being said, UX design is more than the sum of its parts. The process is less about surveys, affinity mapping, and wireframing than it is about understanding why and when to implement them. Now don't get me wrong, they each have their place in the UX design toolkit but we are more interested in the resulting gestalt.

I like to look at things as a whole before I dive into the details. The big picture helps me to put things into perspective, and perspective is the cornerstone of *The Rainbow Stack*. Before I drone on about my process, it would be remiss for me not to share the processes that other designers may use because, as you'll soon see, they're pretty much all the same; it's just a matter of how we choose to butter the bread.

Some designers use what I like to call the *mood-board approach*. They scour the internet looking to strike inspirational gold. For those of you who may not know, a mood board is a type of visual presentation conveying, for want of a better word—a mood. You can accomplish this through media, like text and pictures, but for the scope of this book, media can be replaced with design mockups. Though it does have its purpose, like creating a general reference point for your designs—let's face it we don't live in a vacuum—or keeping abreast of the latest best practices, I'm not a huge fan of this method. I find design processes, which rely heavily on this approach, lack a unique personality and aren't optimized for the job they'll be hired to do. To sum it up, oftentimes they are dazzling to look at but aren't functional, which goes against the principles of good design.

Other designers use *The Elements of User Experience: User-Centered Design for the Web*, written by Jesse James Garrett, whose elements consist of five planes and though created with the web in mind, they translate quite nicely when discussing mobile design.

The five planes are:

1. *Strategy*—The product objectives
2. *Scope*—How the various features all fit together to meet the strategy
3. *Structure*—How the product's information is displayed
4. *Skeleton*—The product's user interface
5. *Surface*—The final product

If I could only use one process this would probably be it, however, the five-plane approach isn't perfect. It does a great job of helping to modularize the design process, which is invaluable, but ultimately it does not exhaustively focus on all of the relevant techniques we'll need along our UX journey. Obviously, this is a very small nitpick but, I think it's worth mentioning as this might be frustrating for beginners.

Others use the *Design Thinking Process* to get the ball rolling. It consists of five straightforward phases:

1. *Empathy*—Understanding the user and designing with them in mind
2. *Define*—Creating a clear problem statement to guide you throughout the design process
3. *Ideation*—The "judgment-free" phase tasked with creating possible solutions
4. *Prototype*—A version of the final product used to turn ideas into tangible assets
5. *Test*—Observing the target users as they interact with the prototype (Waloszek, 2012)

For a designer hopeful, just starting out, I strongly recommend this method. Again, I only have one nitpick when it comes to its implementation; I've found many entrepreneurs often don't start with empathy. While a solid argument can be

THE RAINBOW STACK

made for why they should, out in the real world, they usually start with ideas. So, instead of trying to alter the way many of them work, I prefer a different approach.

Whip up a delicious blend of all of the above-mentioned methods; that is, process reconciliation meets relevant design techniques. If this sounds like a mouthful, don't worry—keep reading.

The
Foundation

HYPOTHESES

"Everyone has to start somewhere."

—Haruki Murakami

Every project starts with an idea. Some of these ideas are often fueled by a myriad of things, call them: product—market fit, *build it and they will come* syndrome, destiny, or a stroke of genius, to name a few. You might hear these ideas being supported by hunches, gut feelings, personal experiences, or even sneaky suspicions. Whatever the rationale, they can, and should, be defined as hypotheses. Why—you ask? Because simply put, hypotheses can be tested, but I'm getting ahead of myself.

At this point you might be wondering, "Okay, what is a hypothesis and where do I get one of those?" Well, if we get a little technical, a hypothesis is a supposition made on the basis of limited evidence as a starting point for further investigation. To bring it home, in the case of *The Rainbow Stack*, these are a series of deductions, a priori or otherwise, upon which the foundation of the product ought *not* to be built. Remember, though essential, they are raw and untested precursors to the final product. Only once proofed, will they help lay the groundwork upon which you will create the perfect user experience.

It is worth mentioning that hypotheses almost always sound logical and reasonable. This makes them especially dangerous as the absence of evidence is *not* evidence of absence. In other words, not being able to find fault with the hypothesis—let's say "the world is flat" doesn't make the world any less round. Hypotheses should always be approached with a healthy skepticism and thoroughly tested before any mockups are designed. To reiterate they are only meant to be a guide and should not influence our build decisions or steer our design strategy.

Context is everything. Throughout the book, I will juxtapose theory with an example of a music streaming service. I find that using a live example better helps to mold these new, alien concepts into something a little more concrete.

For the music streaming app, my initial hypotheses were:

1. End users will pay for a music streaming service
2. Artists will allow their music to be streamed on the platform for free
3. An underserved market is a ready market

These assumptions don't have to be on the money or in the ballpark, as each subsequent iteration through the design process will get us closer to our mark.

EMPATHY

"Two for me. None for you."

—Twix

Our mission should we choose to accept it is to uncover the hidden pain points, that our users are likely to encounter, either right away—or at some point later along their journey, and eliminate them. I like to think of it as Mission Possible. Another way of looking at it is by using a refinement plant analogy. Our hypotheses will be our raw materials, sourced from everywhere. They are rough, coarse, and full of contaminants; but without them, our dream of having a beautifully refined final product will forever go unfulfilled. Next is the empathy stage, which can be thought of as the screener. Its job is to help filter the good from the bad hypotheses. Well, hold on a sec. What's a bad hypothesis and what rubric do we use to make this discernment?

The best way I've found to describe this is by using a quote from Harper Lee's novel *To Kill a Mockingbird*, "You never really understand a person until you consider things from his point of view ... until you climb into his skin and walk around in it." What does this have to do with design? The answer is *everything* and this is the idea of user empathy.

What would the design process look like without empathy? To answer this question, we're going to look again at the streaming app example.

- *Goal*: A dedicated app that streams a single genre of music
- *Outcome*: A modern, "sexy" surface design—think Spotify meets local market
- *Functionality*: What I think makes a great music app, which would include the minimum number of screens needed to cover the basic functionality of such an app, such as playlist creation, audio controls, basic artist information, account details, and curated content

I know what you're thinking—it seems like an okay-ish solution, but not so fast—wait until we add empathy into the mix. Through the lens of user empathy, we then begin to see a vastly different, more complete picture unfold. To get started, let's slowly pour in a few basic empathy-rich questions: What? For whom? and How?

Asking *what* doesn't really change the goal at this point, so the mission remains to design a dedicated app that streams a single genre of music. Nothing earth-shattering here.

The game-changer typically rears its head when we ask *for whom*. If you recall our earlier hypotheses, the streamer would pay to use the service and the musician would allow their music to be used gratuitously, with attribution. Taking a closer look, we seem to be focusing on one user, the streamer, while neglecting to consider the other player in the room. It's at this point some red flags should begin to show up; something is rotten in the state of Denmark. It is becoming rather evident that we hadn't deeply considered who exactly our users will be and what they might want.

Asking *how* can affect the overall design outcome as the goalpost may move if we uncover more information about our users. For example, our initial assumption, of only having to cater to a single user, turns out to be incorrect. We have at least two users, on different sides of the platform, who likely have very different needs. One wants to stream music and the other ostensibly wants to give their masterpieces away for free or be paid for them—we'll determine which soon enough. Figuring out *how* this should work is a little tricky and requires a little bit of careful thought. For instance, by doing some extra digging we should be able to uncover at least two hidden assumptions.

The first is that:
1. The culture of the target users is one that encourages the spending of money on music streaming.

The other is that:
2. Musicians will allow their music to be streamed freely in exchange for exposure.

The sucky thing about these hidden assumptions, besides the fact that they might be way off the mark, is that they sneakily subvert our process as *we can't test what we can't see*. Not to worry, these once hidden assumptions will be tested during our strategy phase.

To wrap things up, let's revisit our initial hypotheses but this time squeeze in a bit of empathy:

1. End users will use a genre-dedicated music streaming service for convenience
2. Artists will allow their music to be streamed on the platform for a price

DEFINE

"Relevance to the real world is what separates innovation from invention."

—Erika Hall

Aah, sweet success; we finally made it through talking about all those troublesome feelings. We finally get to jump into the meat of our design, right? Not so fast—now we have to define our problem. Wait, didn't we start off by defining our problem or, at the very least, the problem that was inferred from our hypotheses?

Yes, however, let's back up a bit. I've tried to make *The Rainbow Stack* as lean as possible; nothing goes to waste. If we don't uncover any insight from a previous stage that can be applied to a subsequent one then there is no reason to include it into the final process. So, we need to ask, what have we learned from the empathy phase?

I know if we were to use the *Design Thinking* jargon it'd be called the define phase, but I like to think of this as the *Re-define* stage. This is the make or break point where we, based on our newfound empathetic insight, determine if we should continue on our design path or pivot. I first read about pivoting from Eric Ries' book, *The Lean Startup*, and highly recommend giving it a read. According to Ries, pivoting is "changing course with one foot anchored to the ground" (Ries, 2011). So, the overarching vision doesn't necessarily have to change for the product to go through a round of optimizations. Fortunately, at this point, we haven't uncovered anything that warrants a sharp pivot but our eyes are wide open.

Using what we've uncovered during the empathy phase we can create an initial problem statement. The *Problem* statement frames the problem in such a way that it creates a foundation that can be easily built upon during the design process. I don't typically spend too much time trying to figure this out here, as it will be proofed during the strategy stage. To start things off, I typically use the following structure:

[Target Users] need [Untested Value Proposition] because [Empathetic Hypothesis]

So, using the music streaming concept, let's try this out:

- "Streamers need an easy way to search, play, and share their favorite music because convenience means control at your fingertips."
- "Artists need to increase their reach potential and earn more money from their music because they deserve it."

From the above problem statements, armed with our measly one design approach, we might begin to feel a little inadequate. To combat this, we might hedge our bets on the idea of creating separate platforms, one for each user. Now if I were a gambling man, I'd take that bet but I'm not, so I won't. We will need something less nuanced to spur us into design action. Think about it another way: Without guiding principles, what would prevent us from re-designing on a whim? For one thing, we'd probably never complete our projects.

Anyway, give yourself a pat on the back as we've come quite a long way in a relatively short time. So, what's next? What's next is my recommendation. Hold onto your shoes because this is where things are going to get a whole lot more interesting.

STRATEGY

"The secret to success is to understand what the real problem is."

—Don Norman

And just like that, we've almost made it out of the design trenches. For all those astute readers who would love to point out a pretty obvious setback, now's your chance. Oh, what's that? Sorry, I can't hear you, so I guess this means we're all good. All jokes aside, if I were to ask you to use what you've learned thus far to start a design process, chances are you wouldn't be able to. Now that's not a knock on you, as theory without the application is like trying to eat steak without teeth; possibly delicious but highly frustrating.

I think we can agree that we're missing a linker, something tangible, a liaison to tie in the theory to the real world. Following the elements of User Experience, the foundation of a successful user experience is a clearly articulated strategy. So, we can safely say, what we're missing are the tools to do the articulating.

We'll be focusing on user needs but there are other members of the *Strategy* plane. We won't be harping on them because while they are important for the project and *The*

Rainbow Stack designer, they are often handed down from upper management—at least in my experience. Before we jump into our UX toolkit, here are a few honorable mentions:

Project Objectives—A set of desired outcomes or statements that relates to the project, which can then be measured by our success metrics. These are super necessary as oftentimes, different people have different ideas as to what the product is supposed to accomplish. In Unger and Chandler's *A Project Guide to UX Design*, they introduce us to probably my favorite term of the entire UX process; *fuzzy objectives*. They are the bane of project objectives, popping up all too frequently and usually taking the form: Our objective is to [insert generic unmeasurable platitude]. A cringe-worthy example for our streaming app could be—our objective is to be the best. Remember project objectives should be easy to understand, distinct, and measurable.

Success Metrics (otherwise known as *UX Metrics*)—A set of pre-established data points used to measure the success of our implementation over time. They ensure the UX design decisions are evaluated using evidence rather than opinions and that we are meeting our project objectives (Garrett, 2010). In other words, they're what we will use to quantitatively determine whether the project was a success. These vary from project to project so we'd have to be sure to ask for them at the start of every engagement; unless of course, you are the decision maker. In such an event, it might be helpful to think of these metrics as key performance indicators (KPIs) with an ascribed threshold for success. It goes without saying that we should try to ensure that these thresholds are as accurate as possible. In the case of our streaming app, our game is attention, that is, how many subscribers are listening to X hours of content per month, where X is the pre-determined minimum threshold for success. This number might be driven by the need to increase ad revenue or to attract investors, but you get the point.

Now, let's talk about user needs. One thing to keep in mind is that we aren't designing for ourselves but rather for the end user. If this concept sounds familiar, it should; this is empathy applied. We will now spend a little time covering some of the necessary tools needed to research and refine those needs, in the hope of breaking the mold of our own parochial silos.

At this point, I'm going to take off the training wheels and say that if you don't understand my explanations, feel free to use an alternate source, more akin to your learning style. Do be sure, however, to follow *why* and *how* the below-mentioned tools are implemented.

Surveys

UX surveys are a relatively easy way to procure relevant information about our potential users. These surveys usually consist of two types of questions: open and closed. I try to stick to the quantitative side of things, asking only closed questions, as my surveys are always multiple choice. I use them as screeners, to filter prospective users from a multitude of generic participants. Keep in mind that a user is not any and everyone, a user is someone who will *use* the final product.

We should avoid, at all costs, asking questions that require our users to speculate. If you find yourself itching to include the proverbial: "If you got [insert feature], would you use my product?", don't. I find that when we start pandering in the hope of getting to *yes*, the dynamic shifts from UX research to a sales pitch and let's be honest, no one likes being pitched. This pitching can lead to the following scenario—The participant infers that you are emotionally attached to your project and they don't want to hurt your feelings by being honest. They respond in the affirmative but really have no intention of following through once the product is built. I call this a false-positive and it's far worse than an outright rejection.

Moving on to the meat and potatoes … instead of going on about the most appropriate survey structure, the best method is for us to create one. Once again, we'll turn to our handy-dandy music streaming app and work through the details. My survey objective is to always identify the right audience with whom I can continue to test my user needs.

We'll start things off with the opener: *Do you listen to [insert genre] music*? We are asking this, as our opening question to weed out any potentially unsavory participants. The choices for this question will either be—*yes* or *no*. If the respondent answers with *no*, we know right away that they will not be one of our users and can screen them accordingly. If they answer in the affirmative we move on to the next question.

I think the most appropriate follow-up question is: *How often?* This cues us in on an important metric—*frequency*. How do users interact with this genre of music? Do they listen every day or is it more seasonal, during a specific time of year? The choices for this question will be every day, every week, every month, a couple of times a year, or once a year.

Next, we'll want to determine which devices our potential users currently utilize to listen to music. I'd phrase this question as: *What is your preferred listening medium*? You might think this is a ridiculously obvious question but hey, if the responses indicate that most of our potential users prefer to listen to their music on vinyl then building a streaming app may not be the right solution for the project. We have a few choice responses for this question: smartphone, tablet, laptop, desktop, or other.

Once we've determined their preferred listening medium, we then need to learn what their experience has been like consuming this content. We don't ask this directly, as there isn't anything useful that can come out of an: "It was nice"—type response. Instead, we want to infer the response from the question: *Which platform do you use to listen to [insert genre]?* By infer, I mean that we can objectively look at the platform they use, to see what their overall experience is like for this particular genre. For example, are there up-to-date pre-made playlists, a healthy array of artists from which to choose, or the ability to easily discover new music? These are really important questions and as such will be investigated further during the interview phase. For now, the choices can be boiled down to the usual suspects: Spotify, Apple Music, Tidal, Google Play Music, YouTube, and generic radio app.

The last question is the closest we'll come to sleight of hand. We want to ask: "Would you pay for our service?" But instead, we'll use some restraint and ask: *Are you currently a subscriber to any streaming services?* This harkens back to our empathy stage when we asked the "how" question. If you recall, we've uncovered at least two hidden assumptions—one of which—Is the culture of the target user, one that encourages spending money on music streaming? Though the final question in our survey doesn't directly answer our once hidden assumption, it's a great place to start as we trod on toward our interviews. To help get to the bottom of this discrepancy, we'll use the following simple combination; either:

1. The culture is one that encourages spending money on streaming and the user
   a. subscribes or
   b. doesn't subscribe
2. The culture is one that doesn't encourage spending money on streaming and the user
   a. subscribes or
   b. doesn't subscribe

In both cases, we're specifically interested in the users who subscribe but more so in the second scenario where, despite the culture, the user buys nonetheless. We can delve further into this esoteric idea of cultural encouragement, by looking at a few factors that contribute to the overall ease of use of subscribing. Are the people in this geographic area used to paying for streaming services? Are credit cards easily available to make the necessary online monthly payments? Are payment gateways allowed to transact business with the local banks? These will ultimately affect our subscription revenue so be prepared to dive into demographics during the interviews.

Last but by no means least, if you're so inclined, I recommend that we send the surveys electronically. It's a hassle-free way to get the ball rolling. What's even niftier is that there's a bevy of free services available to get you started, such as: SoGoSurvey, Typeform, and Google Forms.

Interviews

User interviews are structured conversations with current or potential users of our product. I nabbed my interview structure from the brilliant work of Jake Knapp. In his book,

Sprint: How to Solve Big Problems and Test New Ideas in Just Five Days, he goes over in great detail how to run an efficient and effective user interview. For Knapp's interview method, he implemented a beautifully laid out five-act process. We, however, will only be using the first two acts at this point in *The Rainbow Stack*. Keep in mind that the goal for the first round of our interviews is to obtain a rich set of data, which we can use to create our user personas. Personally, I like to run a second round of interviews, with the full five acts, after completing the Surface plane (more on the Surface plane during *The Build* process).

During Act I, *the friendly introduction*, we start with an easygoing but structured conversation. The goal here is to make the respondent feel as unpressured and relaxed as possible (Knapp et al., 2016). The assumption is that a comfortable environment makes it easier for them to be honest and open. This means small talk with a smile. In the case of our music streaming app, this is the perfect time to follow-up on our demographics question from the survey; be sure to ask the respondent where they're from. Also, it is a great idea to use this time to set the problem context. Once they've gotten past their initial reservations, I like to start with the legal stuff—a document of informed consent—which the respondent has to sign before they can move on. I like to include the purpose of the study, a nondisclosure, permissions, and information we'll be collecting on this one-pager; but, be sure to consult a legal professional before signing off on this document.

During Act II, we ask a series of open-ended context questions about the respondent. Great context questions easily transition from small talk into personal questions relevant to our objective (Knapp et al., 2016). It is important not to ask respondents to speculate on the future, as aspirations make for poor predictors of actual behavior. Also, we must take particular care not to ask leading questions. A leading question is one that uses presuppositions to subtly prompt the respondent to answer in a particular way. This type of question can potentially undermine the entire interview as it could inadvertently confirm our own bias instead of revealing the respondent's beliefs.

Our plan for the interview, or rather the insight we need to uncover, should influence our choice of questions. To be clear, we are searching for the motivation behind their actions, not simply a response. A great place to start is to find out how frequently users are likely to use the app and for how long.

- Do you participate in any activities in which you consider listening to music a must?
- When do you listen to [insert genre]?

Then we need to ascertain how the respondent looks for new [insert genre] music. During this important series of questions, we'll try to uncover any deficiencies or pain points they experience in their quest. This information becomes especially useful when we begin tackling the project scope.

- How do you find new music?
- Being as concise as possible, how would you describe that process?
- Does this service meet your [insert genre] needs?
- How? Why?
- What do you/don't you like about the service?

THE RAINBOW STACK

Last, it's important to thank the respondent for their time and ask if there's anything else they'd like to add. Wasn't that painless? Two things I'd like to point out though:

1. It's important not to rush the respondents out once we get what we're looking for. As tactful designers, this is a must.
2. Throughout the interview, don't always feel compelled to fill the silence with conversation because, as I've discovered, it's really hard to learn with your mouth open.

Oh, and before they go, be sure to give them a gift card or treat, which we used to lure them into the interview.

Typically, if we were doing user research on a single-user product, we'd be done but I hate to break it to you, we're not. Up next, we interview the artist. It can be especially tricky getting a hold of an artist, so we may need to forage for any listed contact details by scrapping their digital channels.

Yes, a little finesse is necessary in order to be successful in getting ahold of an artist for an unsolicited interview. Unless we have the 411 or the inside link, we're probably not going to find their personal contact details. This means any numbers that are unearthed, with a little luck, are likely going to lead to their gatekeeper. Polonius was on to something when he said, "Brevity is the soul of wit." We'll need to grab their attention immediately and keep it, all without coming across as desperate. Here's my approach:

> *We are doing a design research study to determine the feasibility of online music streaming in the [insert geographic location] market. Would [Artist X] be available for a remote interview? We estimate it will take about 7 minutes to complete.*

The worst thing that can happen is that they say, *no*. Okay, I take that back, the worst thing that can happen is getting a typical gatekeeper's false-positive response: "Sounds great, we'll get back to you." So, without being too pushy, counter this response with: "I'd love to follow-up by [insert date] if things get busy and I don't hear back from you guys. How does that sound?"

Assuming we get through, our interview structure should be prepared and ready. We're going to cheat a bit and start with a screener-type question to which we already have the answer. It's far too cumbersome to reliably get ahold of artists, so when we do, we can't afford to leave their suitability to chance. We'll need to do our research beforehand and make certain that their music is on a streaming platform.

- Is your music digitally available online?
- On which platforms?

Next, we assume that the artist hosts their music on a streaming platform to increase their revenue potential, among other things. If they are registered on more than one streaming service, most likely one platform stands dominant over the others. Discovering that platform and what it does well will provide insight into our potential success.

- Which platform is the most financially rewarding for you?
- Is there anything you like or would change about their process?

Last, we'd love to know, if an app existed, which exclusively hosted their genre of music, would they the artist be inclined to use it. Asking this, of course, would be a rookie mistake, violating several of our interview rules.

1. Avoid closed questions if possible
2. Avoid leading questions
3. Avoid pitching

A better strategy is to ask the artist for their opinion on the next logical step for their genre, which we can phrase as follows:

- What do you think are the next steps for [insert genre] as far as technology is concerned?

As with the user interviews, the same rules apply. Thank the artist for their time and ask if there's anything else they'd like to add. This will lead to the conclusion of the interview.

If there's one thing that should be immediately apparent after the interviews, it's that the streamers and the artists have widely different needs. These needs would be extremely difficult to address in a single platform. This cue, if you recall the betting dilemma of our Define phase, constitutes as "that nuance," which is needed to spur us into user platform segregation. It also won't hurt (i.e., strongly recommend) to revise the problem statement so that it more accurately captures the ideal user's frustration.

Next on our design hit list, is the creation of the user personas. But wait, there's one more thing. If after the interviews we realize that what we originally planned to create isn't what our ideal users want, then it's time to pivot. Pivot and pivot again until you get this fit right. There's nothing worse than successfully building the product that we set out to, only to discover that it's a product that doesn't meet the needs of our target audience.

User Personas

A user persona is a fictional representation of our ideal customer. They are used as a constant reminder of our users' needs. They help paint a very clear picture of who will be using the product and potentially how they'll be doing so. It's important to make the distinction between marketing personas, which model purchasing behavior (ew); and UX personas, which model usage behavior. The structure of the persona is pretty standard; I've created a nifty little acronym to get us off to the races. I call it *HEDS* or Header, End Goal, Demographics, and Scenario.

The *Header* kicks off the persona show. The header includes a fictional name accompanied by an equally fictional image, as well as a quote summarizing what matters most to the persona, as it relates to our product. What's great about this part of the persona, is that we don't have to burn any brain cells trying to fill in these fields. For the name, we can use an online name generator and for the image, we can use attribution-free (though we should always give attribution where we can) stock photo websites like Unsplash[1] or Pexels[2]. Personally, I prefer creating the persona image using my favorite vector graphics editor but this is optional. If you'd like to try the do-it-yourself approach, but don't know where to start, Pablo Stanley has a really cool avatar library[3] for Sketch. To complete the header, we need to snag a memorable quote, from our interviews, something that epitomizes the essence of our persona's problem. Though at this point, it might be easy to dismiss the header as overtly useless, it will do a solid job of keeping us focused on our ideal customer.

Up next is the *End Goal*. This can quite simply be explained as the thing that spurs the user into action. It motivates our persona to use our product in order to accomplish their main objective, whatever it may be. In the case of our music streaming app, the uncovered end goal of our users is to: *Discover an easy way to search, play, and share my favorite [insert genre] music*. For the artist, however, this is a little different and by a little, I really mean a lot. Their goal is to: *Increase my reach potential and earn more from my music*.

The third slice of the persona pie, the *Demographics*, is a little more involved. It brings together several moving parts, which eventually fit snuggly into a single profile. Unlike the header, the demographics shouldn't contain any liberal interpretations of the truth. Its moving parts should consist of a user's personal and professional background, respectively, their user environment, and their psychographics.

In the personal background section, we can include a mix of age, gender, ethnicity, education, and status. Whereas in the professional background section, we can include brief employment, details such as occupation, income level, and work experience. We then move on to the user environment, which consists of the context where the user physically uses the product and how they ultimately consume it. I understand this "environment" talk might seem a bit abstract so to bring it home, here's an example.

The user might consume our content by streaming music *on their mobile phone*, during their *daily commute to the office* or *while working out*.

The italicized text highlights the key details of the user environment.

Last is the psychographics section. While demographics explain who our users are, psychographics help us identify why they use our product. Psychographics capture the user's values and activities while mapping their interests and opinions. If at this point we begin to feel that more ice-breaking small talk should have been included during our interviews, then they probably should have. We need to uncover a myriad of details, even ones that may seem insignificant, from how critical our offering is to their everyday life to what types of convictions they might hold. Remember, it's better to collect too much information rather than too little, only to realize our shortcoming while creating our User Personas. Provided we have everything we need then it's on to the scenario, if not—have no fear, we'll just have to redo a few interviews. And yes, feel free to recycle previous participants.

The final piece of the persona puzzle is the *Scenario*. Geoffrey Moore, in his masterpiece *Crossing the Chasm*, does an amazing job of describing a step-by-step blueprint for creating scenarios or as we'll learn to call them—*A Day in the Life Before (the product)*. According to Moore, there are five elements we'll need to address:

1. *Scene or situation*: Focus on the moment of frustration. What is going on? What is the user about to attempt?
2. *Desired outcome*: What is the user trying to accomplish? Why is this important?
3. *Attempted approach*: Without the new product, how does the user go about the task?
4. *Interfering factors*: What goes wrong? How and why does it go wrong?
5. *Economic consequences*: So what? What is the impact of the user failing to accomplish the task productively? (Moore, 1999)

As in the case of the psychographics, we should be able to glean this information from our interviews, either directly or via a series of inferences. Once the questions have been adequately answered, we will have created our guiding light. This light will be used to help illuminate one of our final objectives: to understand—*A Day in the Life After (the product)*. Although not formally part of the user persona, designing with the knowledge of how our user's life could look with our product is an invaluable asset. I can't stress this enough, context is everything!

So, how do we start this particular process? Moore describes "A Day in the Life After (the product)", as taking the same situation and desired outcome from "A Day in the Life Before," but replaying the scenario with our product in place. In this instance, we only need to address three elements:

1. *New approach*: With the new product how does the end user go about the task?
2. *Enabling factors*: What is it about the new approach that allows the user to get unstuck and be productive?
3. *Economic rewards*: What costs are avoided or benefits gained? (Moore, 1999)

Last, we'll need to create personas, as well as *A Day in the Life After* scenarios, for each disparate user we uncover. And that's it; we're done with the foundation of *The Rainbow Stack*. Before we move on to "The Idea Factory," however, it's useful to run through a visual summary of what we've learned thus far.

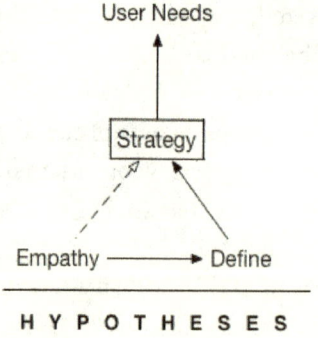

HYPOTHESES

- The hypothesis is the foundation of the process. It is the initial spark that spurs us into action. Most ideas in the real world start here, oftentimes with a: "Wouldn't it be cool if …"
- Up next is the empathy stage, the heart of the process. This is where we climb into the skin of our user and walk around in it for a bit. It helps us to understand the user and refine our hypotheses.
- Empathy influences our Define process. This is where we create our Problem statement; the thing we hope to solve—it helps frame the problem in a way that can easily be designed upon.
- Finally, there's our Strategy plane. It's our launching pad, influenced by our Define process. This is where we bring out the big guns of our UX toolkit to unearth our user needs.

Notes

1. https://unsplash.com/
2. https://www.pexels.com/
3. https://avataaars.com/

The
Idea Factory

IDEATE

"Every game is a world which evolves in stages"

—Dave Gray

We've just moved on from our very first foundation; there were hard times and there were fun times. The journey was far from perfect but we were comfortable. Comfort has this way of breeding a false sense of security, oftentimes preventing us from reaching our full objectives. That's why, deep down, we know that in order to grow we have to keep moving.

A few left swipes later and we've met someone new, their name is Ideate and they're radical, fresh, and different. Though this probably isn't where we'll settle forever, it's perfect for right now.

The ideation phase is a judgment-free zone where we can amble into the unexplored recesses of our creative mind, to explore new possibilities all while thinking outside the box. So, what makes Ideate so especially alluring? It's one of those rare gems that accepts all of us, even our old baggage. Together with our user needs (old baggage), we'll begin to sow the seeds that will eventually lead to our solution.

I think it's safe to say we understand the purpose of the ideation stage, so we should probably stop the analogy here; before things get a little weird. We're going to take our user needs and mix them into a few techniques, which we'll discuss presently, and cook up more than our fair share of ideas. Some of these will be great and some won't be so great and that's okay; our aim is to generate ideas. You're probably wondering how we'll distinguish the good ideas from the bad ones. To be frank, we won't have to, at least not yet. We'll deal with the business of deciding which ideas we should run with when we get to that point. Again, not to flog a dead horse or anything but, our aim now is solely to generate unique ideas.

As we drill deeper into the Ideate stage, things are going to become a lot less *template-y*. Unlike the foundation stage where we had the ability to be quite formulaic with our approach, we no longer have that luxury. The open-ended questions we asked in our interviews, to discover our user, will inevitably lead to a lot of variation. In other words, what works for my data may not work for yours, so understanding the necessary techniques to navigate this section is going to be more important than ever.

Gamestorming

We can't discuss idea generation without first having a conversation about the idea generation factory; the gamestorm. In its simplest form, gamestorming is a set of structured rules used to generate a kaleidoscope of innovative ideas; the key to the black box of creativity.

In their book, *Gamestorming—A Playbook for Innovators, Rulebreakers, and Changemakers*, Dave Gray and his band of codifiers put together an exhaustive list of techniques to ensure that the idea generation factory is forever bursting at its seams. We'll briefly cover the basic tenets of gamestorming while diving into a few examples. Don't worry; we'll only go over a few, which relate to our music streaming example for the following reasons:

1. Gamestorming is not the purpose of this book
2. There are far too many options to cover
3. I'd rather not lose your attention (if I haven't already)

Gamestorming can be explored using five types of core questioning. We, however, will become familiar with the techniques through opening, exploration, and closing games.

Games for openings are used to generate ideas, to provoke thought, and reveal possibilities; think of it as a jump-start for our creative mind (Gray et al., 2010).

The first game I always begin with is the *anti-problem*. It tasks us with solving the problem, which is opposite of our current problem. This is a solid place to start because, in order to know what we should be creating, it's also important to know what we shouldn't. Continuing with the example, let's look at our *streamer*. Their problem is lack of control and convenience when attempting to listen to the music they love. So, during the anti-problem, our job is to figure out how to make their music streaming experience as restrictive and inconvenient as possible. In so doing, besides having a lot of fun, we'll learn to evaluate the problem differently and break out of any existing mental models.

Next is one of my favorite opening techniques, the *pre-mortem*. It's great learning from our mistakes but wouldn't it be better if we didn't have to burn to learn? The purpose or pre-mortem is to directly address potential risks, at the beginning of the Ideation stage, before they have a chance to materialize. To get started, evoke Murphy's Law by asking the simple question: "How will this potentially end in disaster?" Perhaps, too few paying streamers will subscribe to the service, which will result in insufficient revenue generation. Thus, the artists will be inadequately compensated for their music and forced to abandon the platform. This sounds good but here come those pesky red flags again. You're probably wondering, what's the point of uncovering this issue if we aren't addressing its solution. Well, I only use pre-mortems to unearth issues that can potentially derail the project in its current form. The would-be solution will be converted into a requirement that will rear its head during the Scope phase. Last, we should list all the uncovered risks and rank their perceived priority, before we close this exercise.

So, we've successfully navigated past some opening techniques, however, we're not quite at the closing. We're somewhere smack-dab in the space between; this is where we begin our exploration. Games for exploration help us assess our course, point the way forward, and adjust for error (Gray et al., 2010).

I prefer to start the exploration process with affinity mapping. Affinity maps help us organize the raw data and ideas we've collected, during the interview process, into groups. We can then use these organized groups to uncover deeper insights or trends from our user research. Why do we want to do this? Well for starters, it's a pretty painless and effective method for sorting all the qualitative data we've collected. Furthermore, it has the potential benefit of helping us uncover hidden themes or patterns among our end users. To get started we'll need to transcribe all the notes and observations, obtained from our user interviews, to a large working surface, digital or otherwise. Then we'll sort similar data (data that share common themes) into groups and give each group a name. Last, we'll attempt to glean some key insights from each of the newly formed groups. Key insights are simply statements about what we've learned from each grouping. Okay, how do we know if we've nailed our key insights? I've found that an affirmative answer to the following question is the perfect indicator:

Do our insights reveal that the problem we're trying to solve was created by the solution to an older problem?

It is worth noting that these insights will also inform our scope.

Next, we move on to the Lean Canvas—a one-page business plan template created by Ash Maurya that helps to deconstruct our ideas into their key assumptions. We'll repurpose the Lean Canvas a bit, since our assumptions have already been proofed at this point. So, the Lean Canvas's newly repurposed function will be to help us formalize our ideas by giving them structure. Gray and company (2010) suggest using the Business Model Canvas; but, I've found the repurposed Lean Canvas better suited to my Rainbow Stack needs. To complete the canvas, we must populate all of its nine segments. Though we won't go over them all, if you've been following along, there should be little issue in sourcing the necessary information.

First up are the customer segments. This data can be easily pasted in from the Demographics section of our interviews.

Then we can tackle the Problem section; this is where up to three uncovered user problems, as well as any market competitors are listed. We can snatch our user problem-related key insights, from our affinity map, to satisfy the problem requirement. We then use our *A Day in the Life (Before)*, from the user persona, to list how these problems are currently solved today. The last of the copy-and-paste sections, is the Unique Value Proposition section or UVP. The UVP is a clear, compelling message that states why it's worth paying attention to us. I've found a good place to start is by framing the interview-validated problem statement as a list of itemized benefits to our soon-to-be proposed solution.

1. **Control.** Every [insert genre] song at your fingertips
2. **Convenience.** Easily search, play, and share your favorite [insert genre] music
3. **Freedom.** Take [insert genre] with you wherever you go

We then make an easy-to-follow, relevant, high-level X for Y analogy: Think Spotify but only for [insert genre] music. It goes without saying that this example relates only to the streaming user and we'll need to repeat the procedure for the artists.

To wrap things up, we'll fill in the remaining sections with our best guess until we reach the testing phase, as our subsequent responses will now be based on our subjective opinion and not necessarily those verified by research. Once the entire Lean Canvas is mapped out we can then assess its strengths and weaknesses. Be on the lookout for any recurring, problematic themes.

Closing games serve the opposite function from opening games. They are instrumental in helping us focus and converge our selection (Gray et al., 2010).

A great place to start is with the *NUF* test. We're going to use it as a quick reality check on the ideas we've generated thus far. Grading our ideas is the first step in filtering the good ideas from the bad ones. During the NUF test, the quality of our ideas is rated based on three criteria: their *Novelty*, their *Usefulness*, and their *Feasibility*. The ratings go from zero to ten and the higher the rating the more novel, useful, or feasible the idea. At the end of a typical NUF test, a quantitative

THE RAINBOW STACK

(though subjective) graded measure of our most important ideas should come out. If for any reason following your gut feeling to make scoring decisions just doesn't cut it, there's always the *Analytic Hierarchy Process*. This process uses linear algebra techniques to objectively list our ideas from best to worst. So, how does this NUF test actually work? Well, we begin with the criteria:

- *Novelty*—Has the idea been tried before?
- *Usefulness*—Does the idea accurately solve a problem?
- *Feasibility*—How easily can it be implemented?

We then take our criteria and create a matrix against our ideas. The criteria become the column titles and the ideas, the row titles. Thus, each idea receives a rating when measured against a single criterion. The ratings are tallied and the highest-rated idea is the winner. Conversely, the lowest-rated idea is the loser. However, we don't give up on losers here so our next task is to ask ourselves: "How do we make this idea more NUF?"

To round out our abridged gamestorming session, there is the *Start, Stop, Continue* game. It is as easy as it is straightforward and functions as either an opening or closing game. I prefer to implement it at the end because it helps to focus our ideas through perspective. As the name implies, it contains three sections: *start*, *stop*, and *continue*. During the Start section, we need to ask ourselves: What are some things our product should be doing? Likewise, during the Stop section, we ask the opposite: What might our product do that it shouldn't? Yes, I'm aware this is all highly speculative but that's the point; so, don't dismiss it. Last, during the Continue process, we ask ourselves: What might our product do that it should continue to do?

And that's it, we're done. Though it might seem like quite a lot, we've merely scratched the surface. I encourage you to research as many gamestorming techniques as you can to determine the most suitable one for your particular project.

So, now that we've generated all our unique, crazy, on-point, off-the-mark ideas, what do we do with them? How do we decisively select the *winning-est* ideas upon which we can build our prototype? This is the perfect time to introduce the *Scope* and the *Structure* or as I like to call them collectively, the *Editor*. The Scope is where the initial culling is made while the Structure is where our ideas are formatted into visual flows.

SCOPE

**"It's not about volume or detail.
It's about clarity and accuracy"**

—Jesse Garrett

Oftentimes, a product can simply be described as a series of features. Though not incorrect, I think we can add to this definition by appending: ... *that serve to solve a specific set of use cases, uncovered by user needs*. This is not done to be overly pedantic but rather to slay the amorphous amalgam that is the feature set, by imposing constraints. How do we do this? Well, if you've ever heard the terms *functional specifications* or *user requirements*, this is where they are created and implemented.

If you're unfamiliar with these terms, functional specs or user requirements define the boundaries of what the user expects the product to be able to do.

When crafting these requirements, we need to ensure that we include solutions to the deficiencies, or pain points, uncovered during our customer interviews and fully develop via our gamestorm. This includes any potential solutions discovered as a result of our pre-mortem exercise as well as helpful key insights from our affinity map. Turning once again to our music streaming example, we're going to use one of the potential problems raised during our pre-mortem, to find a suitable solution upon which to build a healthy requirement. If you recall, we suspected that: if paying streamers, subscribing to the service, were to fall below a set anticipated threshold, the result will be the inability of the service to cover its costs. One immediately obvious solution is to increase overall revenue. How could we do this? Well, there are a few ways, one of which is to seek out paying advertisers. We can create tiered advertiser fees in exchange for displaying their respective banner ads and possibly playing commercials between songs.

So, we've uncovered a problem and found a viable solution. Great, now we just need to write up a quick requirement and move on to the next problem, right? Well, not so fast! Knowing this is just half the battle as we can't just start writing requirements all willy-nilly. To get things off the ground, there are a few rules that need to be adhered to. Following the *Elements of User Experience*, they are: *be positive*, *be specific*, and *avoid subjective language*.

Be positive sounds like a self-help aphorism but it actually deals with effective communication. The goal is to convey the requirements as succinctly as possible, however, by describing what the product shouldn't do, doesn't explicitly tell us what it should. Let's take for example the log-in screen. Instead of the seemingly acceptable requirement:

The user will not be allowed to log in to the app without an account

We might consider rewriting it as:

The user will be prompted to sign up if they attempt to log in without an account

THE RAINBOW STACK

Pretty subtle, but highly effective. Next, is to *be specific*. Again, one of the goals for writing our requirements is to communicate them in a way that leaves no room for doubt. In other words, leave as little as possible open to interpretation. What does this look like? Well, I'm glad you asked; let's look at another example.

The most popular artists will be highlighted on the user's profile

The above-mentioned requirement actually raises more questions than it answers and this is our first indication that it is not specific enough. What rubric will be used to determine popularity? What is a highlight? Instead, we might consider:

Artists whom the user has listened to the most, over the last week, will appear on a Top 10 list, on the user's profile

Though a little wordier, the above requirement defines its purpose in specific detail. The last rule on the list is to *avoid subjective language*. If you're sensing a theme here, you're right on the money. Concision is our goal. This is yet another way of removing any ambiguity from the process.

The interface will be super cool and awesome

Besides being extremely fuzzy, this requirement is hinged on subjective language. After all, what exactly does it mean to be "super cool" or "awesome?" Like the project objectives we encountered in our strategy section, requirements must be falsifiable. Put another way, if we can't prove them wrong, how can we know if the requirement has been met?

You're probably wondering: Are there any questions we can ask to help salvage this requirement? Fortunately, the answer, in most cases, is *yes*. We just have to coerce the details out a bit.

- What does it mean to be "super cool?"
- What does "super cool" look like?
- Why is it important for the interface to be cool?
- Does epitomizing this coolness benefit the app?
  - If so, how?

We have to drill down into the details and pull out the healthy requirements. If not, we run the risk of introducing our product to scope creep. Let's face it, no one likes a creep and our product is no exception.

STRUCTURE

"Just because you can't see it, doesn't mean it's not there."

—Louis Rosenfeld

The *Structure* is the bridge that connects the Scope to the Prototype. You're probably wondering: How do we take words, in the form of requirements, and create visual elements? The simple answer is, we format them.

We'll begin by developing a conceptual structure for our product, which will determine what our users will ultimately experience. The process for accomplishing this is loosely brought to the fore through *Information Architecture*. Sticking as close to the basic definition as possible, Information Architecture deals with the options involved in conveying information to a user, that is, creating architectural maps and user flows. However, being the design renegades that we are, we'll peer under the surface, just a bit, to catch a glimpse of what lies beneath the definition *hood*.

In their eponymous book, *Information Architecture*, the authors—Louis Rosenfeld and company, define it as follows:

1. The structural design of shared information environments.
2. The synthesis of organization, labeling, search, and navigation systems within digital, physical, and cross-channel ecosystems.
3. The art and science of shaping information products and experiences to support usability, findability, and understanding.
4. An emerging discipline and community of practice focused on bringing principles of design and architecture to the digital landscape. (Rosenfeld et al., 2015)

Yes, I'll admit this is a bit of a mouthful but it's one of the better, more complete definitions I've come across.

Now, there are a few ways to cross the structure bridge; for example, Jesse Garrett provides an online visual vocabulary that dives into extraordinary detail. Though a solid resource, I don't think it's the best place, for beginners, to start when trying to get to prototype land. A lot is being thrown at us, right out of the gate, and it might be a little overwhelming for some. That being said, once we become more experienced in the field, this is definitely a library worth exploring. It will, most notably, help us to better articulate our architectural maps and task flows.

I always begin the crossing with *mind maps*. A mind map is a hierarchical diagram that visually organizes information. It is the first tool that I employ to add structure to my requirements. I usually list all the requirements on a sheet of paper or in a Word document, and then categorize them by theme. These categories will eventually go on to become pivotal

THE RAINBOW STACK

nodes, where they'll be structurally connected to other related requirements, which I call the *branches*.

I could sing all day about the inner marvels and workings of the mind map, but it won't necessarily make the concept any easier to comprehend. I think the best thing to do is to work through an actual example. Let's begin with the category requirements.

The app will allow users to:

1. Play their favorite [insert genre] music as individual songs or within playlists
2. Search our database to easily find artists, curated playlists, and songs
3. Customize and create playlists of any length
4. Share music with friends

Though I must admit this example is somewhat oversimplified, let's get Kraken.

In the illustration above, we took the verbs from our requirements and used them as the cornerstone of our categories. I know it's probably difficult to contain your excitement; but, we're not out of the woods just yet. The next task is to ask ourselves: How do we further develop our mind map? To answer this question, a brief refresher on grammar rules is needed.

To build on our fledgling map, we need to first identify and include similar developing ideas. These might take the form of other requirements or, as is the case in our basic example, the adverbial clause of the requirement in question. Remember an adverbial clause is a dependent clause—a fancy word for a sentence fragment that answers the question: How, why, or under what conditions did the action, of the sentence, take place? For example, how does the user play their favorite [insert genre] music? The answer is: As an individual song or within playlists. This is then what is used to create and connect our map branches.

Last, we repeat this process for all the category requirements.

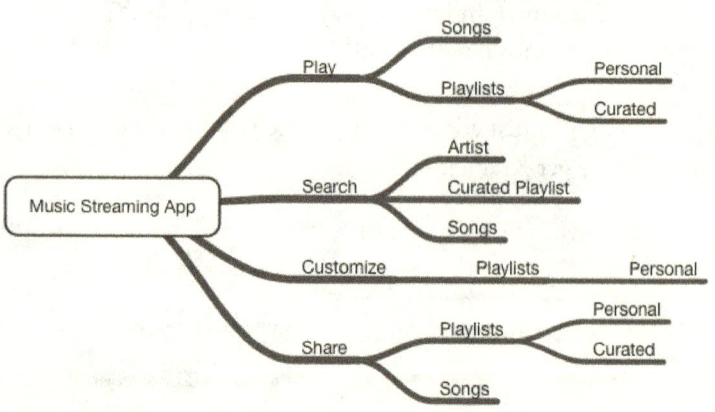

Now that our requirements have been given structure, where do we go from here? We move on to the *user journey map*. According to the Nielsen Norman Group (NN/g), "A [user or customer] journey map is a visualization of the process that a person goes through in order to accomplish a goal. It helps illustrate our persona's experiences as a sequence of steps" (Gibbons 2018).

THE RAINBOW STACK

As a welcomed corollary, journey maps also aid in providing a unique perspective: that of the outsider looking in. It is, therefore, reasonable to assume that journey maps should be used during the empathy phase or at least during our opening gamestorm. I disagree for two reasons: The first is that we simply just don't know enough about the user during the empathy stage. The second is that during the gamestorm, we haven't yet consolidated our thoughts into requirements, so I find using them here, to be a bit premature. Journey maps should always be created to support known business requirements.

The basic structure that I employ is to start with broad overarching stages, then break them down into steps, describe their associated story, and end with their emotional toll. The *Stages* section provides a brief outline of where we are in the journey; it sets the scene by giving context. The *Steps* section is a sequence of actions that break down the Stage into touch points. These touch points can be used to create a storyboard, but this is optional and I typically omit this task. The *Story* or text lane, adds additional information and context to our Steps by further describing the user's experience. The *Emotional Journey* shows the user's satisfaction, in graph form, at each step, and is graded on a 5-point scale from +2 to –2.

Based on key insights from our affinity map, we are aware of a few circumstances in which users might find themselves, with a job to do, where our service could be hired to help. These jobs include:

- The workout motivator
- The commute time killer
- The lime starter

Putting our lime starter job in the hot seat, let's go through an example of what a journey map might look like. Before we go any further, however, let's address the elephant in the room. A *lime* in this instance is not a round citrus fruit, but is instead local Caribbean parlance for a gathering of persons with the express intent of hanging out.

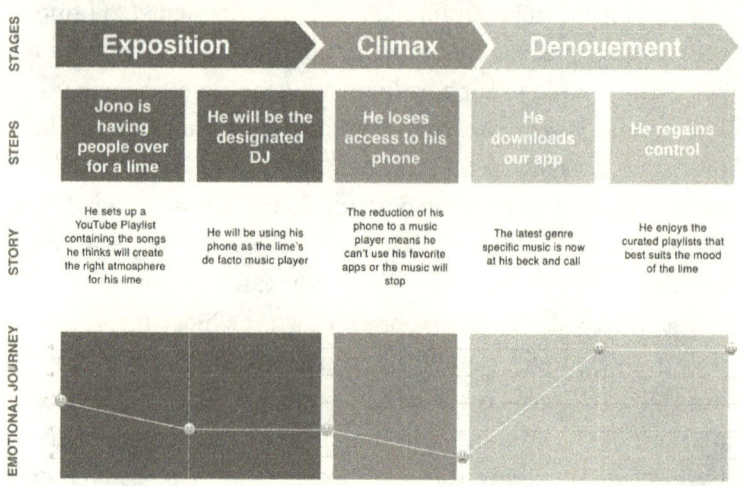

In the first act, Jonathan Peters is having friends over. He sets up a YouTube playlist containing the songs he thinks will create the right atmosphere for his lime. He is the designated DJ, which means he'll need to use his phone as the lime's de facto music player. The exposition finds Jono going from emotionally neutral to slightly frustrated.

In the second act, things heat up as Jono loses access to his phone. His phone is reduced to a brightly lit music player. If he tries to use any of his favorite apps during this time, the music will stop. Needless to say, Jono's emotional state goes from slightly to highly frustrated.

THE RAINBOW STACK

In the final act, Jono discovers our music streaming app and marvels not at its beautiful design, but the fact that it solves his current problem perfectly. He now has dominion over his streaming experience; the music is at his beck and call. With this newfound control, Jono enjoys curated playlists that best suit the mood of his lime. The denouement sees his now famously capricious emotional state go from highly frustrated to aptly satisfied.

Next is the architectural map and the user or task flow. Don't be fooled—though these may seem identical in function at first, they are quite different. The architectural map reveals the visual hierarchy of our product's layout, while the user flow provides details on the various path options available to the user as they navigate the product. With the completion of these two bad boys, we'll finally be ready to saunter along into prototype land.

Architectural mapping is one of those techniques with no logical trickery involved. To begin, we simply take our mature mind map and build on its layout. A common misconception, however, is that the architectural map is supposed to be used as a link documenter. The architectural map's purpose is not to show every link within the product, but rather to show the conceptual relationships. According to Jesse Garrett, in order to strengthen these relationships and make them more apparent we need to ask two questions:

1. Which categories go together, and which remain separate?
2. How do the steps in a given interaction sequence fit together? (Garrett, 2010)

The jobs for which our product will be hired, that is, our use cases, will help influence our response to the aforementioned questions. In all of our use cases, we've found that curated content was mostly used for convenience. Therefore, it served a different set of needs compared to personally created content, which was used for control. This was a dead giveaway that our categories needed to be displayed on separate screens. To see how the steps in the log-in sequence fit together, we'll stick to our lime starter job and focus on the curated side of the map.

Everything we've done thus far, from the interviews to the journey map, suggests that having thoughtfully focused playlists, at the ready, is highly coveted by our users. What does this tell us? For one, it tells us that curated playlists are an important solution to one of our users' biggest pain points. It goes without saying, solutions to these important user pain points should carry a higher than average design weight. The curated playlist therefore should be given a sizeable amount of app real estate. We can even go a step further and say that it should be one of, if not, the first thing the user sees when logging into the app. Though we don't yet know what form the list will ultimately take on, what we do know is that its placement will be contingent upon its ease of consumption by our users.

What else should the user see on their home screen? Fortunately, the days of guessing are behind us, so let's take the information we do have and attempt to answer this question. Users find it difficult to reliably discover new music; either they don't know the artist by name or are unaware of the song title. This inevitable drawback ultimately prevents finding a solution to their problem as quickly as they'd like. One thing to keep in mind is, no matter how intuitive the layout, there'll always be a learning curve for our users. That

THE RAINBOW STACK

being said, we'll try to reduce the friction, as much as possible, by giving the user choices. We'll allow them to search via trending artists, the latest music, as well as the traditional method of searching by text.

The curated side of the app is all about music discovery. So, it makes sense that this screen should be the first thing the user sees. It will consist of curated playlists, a search bar (for text search), a list of trending artists, and the latest released singles.

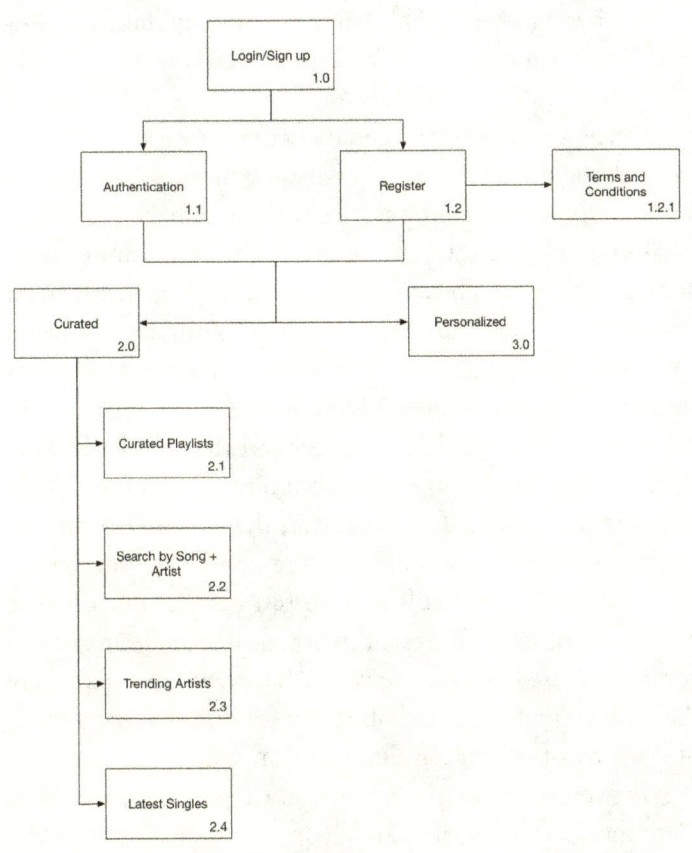

Here are a few things to consider when creating architectural maps:

1. We should try to achieve an even spacing and alignment of our map components. This aesthetic makes our map look more professional and easier to follow.
2. We need to be consistent with font sizes as well as the placement of our text. This makes our map easier to read and use.
3. We should always create maps with a coherent numbering system. This helps remove any lingering flow ambiguity. (Unger & Chandler, 2012)

Fancy a segue? Great, because we're now going to run a small thought experiment. Let's assume that we've nailed the structure of the streaming service with our amazing architectural map. How do we adequately identify the various hierarchical elements? The answer is: we label them correctly. At first glance, this sounds like a winning solution but how do we know if we used technical or otherwise unfamiliar terms throughout the application? More importantly, what do you think will be the result? If you guessed that users will have difficulty navigating the app, congratulations—you get 2 brownie points. It is for this reason that before continuing we need to perform an audit with a controlled vocabulary list. Ultimately, we'll still have to test our list but this is a good place to start. To create this list, we'll compile an array of commonly used, alternative words for every label, especially the ones we're most proud of. If you find it difficult to think of similar words, you can simply use an online thesaurus.

To wrap things up, we'll now move on to the user flow diagram. User flow diagrams help to create a map of the options available to the user as they navigate our product. They are an important development point as we transition toward the prototype stage. Though these diagrams are a little more involved than architectural maps, they shouldn't be too troublesome.

Before illustrating the effectiveness of the user flow diagram, we need to become familiar with the user flow's language. This is done through the use of symbols. Our flow will consist of a few common geometric shapes, which will represent some important steps:

- The *terminator symbol* marks the starting or ending point of the flow—this symbol is represented as a rectangle with rounded corners.
- The *decision node* is a point of choice for the user—this symbol is represented as a diamond.
- The *manual input* is self-evident: If there are any instances when the user will be prompted to enter information manually, a slanted rectangle symbol is used.
- The *subroutine* is used for demarcating a preexisting flow, defined on a separate diagram, indicating a sequence of actions that perform a specific task. We can implement the subroutine on all tasks that aren't immediately relevant. Think of it as a collapsed accordion without the ability to expand; it helps focus our attention by keeping the flow clean and uncrowded. This is symbol is represented as a rectangle within a larger rectangle.
- The *action symbol* is by far the most common of the shapes we'll come across. It can be a single step or an entire subprocess within our flow. This symbol is represented the as a rectangle.

Using a basic example to illustrate the possible steps involved in authenticating a user's account, we'll put into practice the techniques necessary to tackle even bigger flows. We know from our requirements that: *The user will be prompted to sign up if they attempt to log in without an account.* We also know from our architectural maps, the conceptual relationships within the log-in structure. Now that you've been introduced, albeit, briefly to the language of user flow, it's the perfect time to get our hands wet.

The user flow should begin with a prompt to log in. If the user does not have an account they will be directed to a screen where they can register. Then they'll be whisked to the log-in screen, once again, where they can enter their newly minted credentials. Once authenticated, the user will be taken to the curated section of our product, where they can enjoy the service they signed up for; genre-specific music streaming.

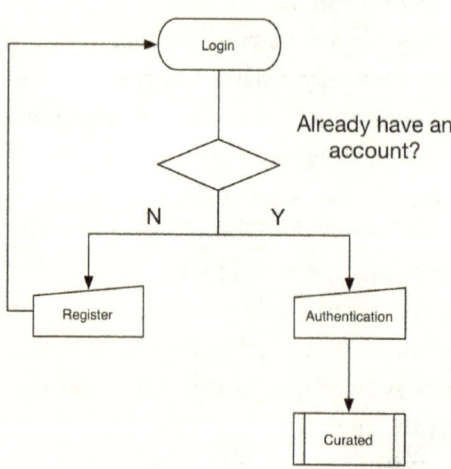

And just like dynamite, boom, that's it, we're done. Pretty straightforward and absolutely essential for converting words into visual elements. This brings us to the end of *The Rainbow*

THE RAINBOW STACK

Stack's "Idea Factory." As we did with the Foundation, before we move on to "The Build," it's useful to run through a visual summary of what we've learned thus far.

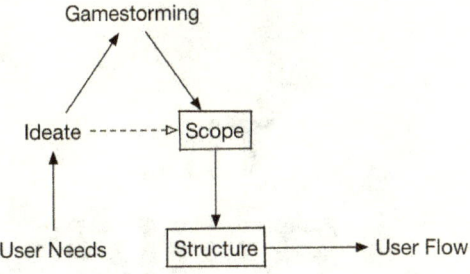

- The user needs are the old baggage that we happily carry around with us, even after we've left our foundation behind. No, it's not sad; we're proud of them as they play an active role in developing our requirements.
- Up next is the Ideation stage. This is an important zone, which frees us from those judgmental eyes, which in turn helps foster a creative environment.
- Gamestorming is made possible through the creative environment set by the Ideation stage. It is a wonderful set of structured rules used to generate the ideas, which will go on to become the basis of our requirements.
- Last, we have the editors: Scope and Structure. The Scope plane is where we decide which ideas make the cut to become one of our next top requirements.
- The Structure plane is the bridge that connects the Scope to the Prototype. It plays an essential role in converting our requirements into visual elements.

The
Build

PROTOTYPE

"Don't differentiate without a difference"

—Andrew Grove

We're getting closer to what our friends think of when they hear the words UX design. If that statement makes you cringe—as it should—that's okay. You see, we've arrived at a very important milestone in our journey. This is where the magic happens. This is where we take our design straws and churn them into gold. We've queued all our raw ingredients, so now we're ready to start working on our chef d'oeuvre.

Okay, hold on a sec. Why do we need a prototype? Don't we already have everything we need to start building our product? The short answer is, *no*, not quite. We know what our users want but not how they'll react to our interpretation of their needs. This is where the prototype comes in—it helps us make more informed design decisions by allowing us to test for potential usability issues. I like to think of this stage as the facilitator, the try-before-you-buy guy. The only difference is the prototype is guaranteed to save us time and money in the long run.

If you're still a little skeptical, imagine hungrily walking through, what appears to be, a luxurious mall. It's designed with everything from filigreed railings and a vaulted glass ceiling to impeccably laid, obsidian, ceramic tiles. Being entoured by all of its decorative pieces is nice but we didn't ask for them and definitely don't need them. We just wanted to grab a cheeseburger, at the Food Court, with a side of fries.

From the very beginning of *The Rainbow Stack*, our goal has been to uncover and solve our users' problems. We began with user needs and, with a little processing, crafted these into visual elements. The prototype stage helps build on these elements, to various levels of fidelity, where they can then be reliably tested. We want to avoid constructing a mall if all our users simply need is a Food Court.

SKELETON

**"Details are the essentials.
The standard to measure quality by."**

—Dieter Rams

If the *Structure* plane is the backbone of the product, then what is the *Skeleton* plane? The Skeleton plane is like the muscular system; it deals with gross motor and fine movement. In other words, the Skeleton plane focuses on the design components with varying levels of detail. It is the beginning of our foray into the development of the user interface.

If you're thinking of user interface as in UI, as in UX/UI, you're right on the money. This however, is a misnomer, as the user interface is *part* of the user experience. So, saying UX/UI is equivalent to ordering a cheeseburger with cheese—it's redundant. Try to avoid this rookie mistake, expel it from our vocabulary, and exclusively use the term *UX*. Now that we've cleared that up, what exactly is this UI?

The textbook definition of UI is the space where interactions between humans (our users) and machines (our product) occur. Yes, it's pretty bland but, nevertheless, it serves its purpose. This interface can be broken down into three "separate" sections. These are *interface design, navigation design,* and *information design*. I know, they sound indiscernibly similar but following Garrett's *Elements of User Experience*, we are provided with a robust rubric to help navigate these relationships.

If it involves:

1. Providing users with the ability to *do things*—it's interface design
2. Providing users with the ability to *go places*—it's navigation design
3. Communicating *ideas to the user*—it's information design (Garrett, 2010)

We will drill into a little more detail to ensure these nuances become more apparent. Once again, let's solidify these concepts by turning to our handy-dandy music streaming example. This time, however, I need you to humor me for a moment. Let's assume, just this once, that the platform is already built.

The first thing users do, after opening the music app, is: sign up. To accomplish this task, they first have to enter their personal data into a series of text fields. Once completed, they hit a fairly prominent call-to-action button and move one step closer to music—*Shangri-La*. Wait a minute—shouldn't a social media authentication button have been included by the designer to save time? Well yes; but, the quality of the experience isn't the point here. The moment users interact with the product by entering data or poking UI elements, they've entered the realm of interface design.

The second thing they'll probably do is find their bearings; tapping on things to explore the new space. Whether or not they find what they're looking for, the ability to move around the app is facilitated through navigation design.

Thanks to navigation design they've made it to the personalized section of the platform. As the name suggests, it will eventually be populated with music that they've added. Does this mean that, at this particular juncture, there is no data on this screen? No, not necessarily. Just because there is nothing to display doesn't mean the screen needs to be devoid of data. An *empty state* is the perfect example of information design. Empty states are temporary parts of the user experience where no user data is available to be displayed. As a result, instead of subjecting the user to a blank screen, thoughtful designers use this opportunity to communicate information.

Wireframing

The wireframe is yet another tool in our design toolkit. It is a visual guide that embodies the essence of the *Skeletal* plane. These are so well-known, we could even go so far as to say, that wireframes are the poster child for the user experience. They convey the form, that is, the shape and configuration, of our user flows. You might be wondering: What about color? On our wireframes, the saturation dial is permanently turned all the way down to zero. Color only comes into play during the Surface plane; for now, we're stuck with black, white, and shades of gray.

Wireframes can be broken up into two main levels of detail: high fidelity and low fidelity. The fidelities are technical terms, which indicate how closely the prototype resembles the final product.

Low fidelity, or Lo-Fi, is often an abstract representation of the product. This is achieved with the use of simple geometric shapes. I'm not aware of a standardized set of rules for Lo-Fi wireframes; however, I have my own preferences. When representing text, for example, rectangles can be used in varying heights to represent font size and varying widths to represent the line length. For good measure, we can use shades of gray to represent the font weight. Again, this isn't set in stone; so, you could potentially use whatever convention works best but it needs to be consistent.

High fidelity, or Hi-Fi, more closely matches the actual level of detail in the final product. Though the layout remains unchanged there are obvious differences when compared to Lo-Fi prototypes. The easiest way to describe this difference is with the use of an analogy, for example, a trip to the ophthalmologist. Picture sitting and looking through a pair of awkwardly positioned lenses, all while having to stare at that smug Snellen chart. In the beginning, everything is a blur but over a few iterations, the indiscernible blocks transform into legible letters. That clarity is the effect that Hi-Fi adds to our wireframe. So, where we might have used a plain old circle and solid fill to represent a user's profile picture, now we may just use a placeholder avatar. It's also worth mentioning that typical type rules such as: kerning, tracking, and line spacing, can be applied here.

On the off chance, that we encounter difficulty adding the final touches to our wireframe, this is the one time to consider utilizing a mood board. We simply fire up our favorite web browser and search for UX screens with similar product analogs. This technique can also be used as part of a competitor analysis. The major difference is, instead of scrounging off mood boards, we'd capture our competitor's delicious user interface through screenshots.

Labeling

As designers, it's important to be cognizant of, not only our role within the realm of the user experience but, our place within the entire development process. The product team, in which UX design plays an integral part, is made up of a bevy of specialties such as engineering, management, and marketing, to name a few. These specialties come together in a very specific way, to make the final product a success. In other words, the order in which tasks are carried out is important. Don't worry, we won't discuss all of these specialties; only that of the person running the subsequent leg. What does this mean? It means, not just eyeing the finish line, but also the next team member we're going to pass to and deliver the product baton. In case you're still wondering, I'm talking about the developer. We only need to be familiar with a tincture of their language to make the handoff a pleasurable experience. Fortunately for us, knowing how our developer thinks doesn't involve any coding.

Though the method we're about to discuss can be applied to any front-end language, we're going to assume our developer codes in React—arguably the most popular JavaScript framework on the planet. React is modular by nature. Thus, a component (block of code) can be rendered on a page on which its source code is not found. This means that the component can be re-used, in separate instances, without ever having to repeat a line of code. How does this extra tidbit help us? Believe it or not, wireframes can be designed in a similar fashion, reducing the chance of any potential handoff friction. Using our streaming service as an example, let's explore what this language familiarity entails.

When creating wireframes, it's standard procedure to employ the use of a few shapes, most notably: the circle and the rectangle. These shapes, by default, are resigned to a life of eponymy (rectangle 1, rectangle 2, etc.), unless we rescue them through thoughtful labeling. When there are more than a few items on a screen, it's easy to see how things can devolve into a school of copy-and-pasted shapes with no identity; the opposite of modular. If this is difficult to picture; you can refer to the left-hand side of the wireframe illustration below.

It's impossible to discern which label corresponds to which parts of the design. To make matters more interesting, the labels are unordered. Now, this wouldn't be such a big deal if we were designing for ourselves but, alas, this is not the case. So, to whip this bad boy into handoff-ready shape, we first need to order the labels (giving them identifiable names doesn't hurt) and group them by related items. Then each group will have to be converted into a symbol—think, a designer's equivalent to a developer's component. Symbols, therefore, are instances of reusable design elements.

The final step entails carefully formatting each symbol so that they mimic our developer's soon to be component. How might we do this? We simply place the capitalized symbol name, accompanied by a backslash, between a pair of angle brackets < SymbolName />. With these changes, we'll save the developer a lot of time and, quite possibly, frustration.

THE RAINBOW STACK

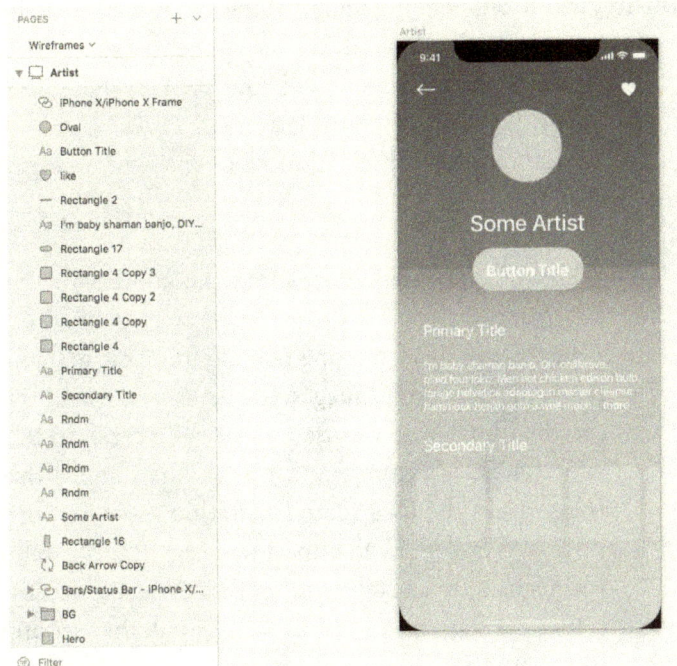

Heuristic Analysis

Before testing our wireframes with real live users, we have to pass our own internal litmus test. This test comes in the form of a checklist, based on best practices, used to evaluate a design's usability. I like to think of it as our very own quality assurance process. During the heuristic analysis, it's likely that both strengths and weaknesses within our wireframes will be uncovered. At this point, we're not too concerned about the things we've done well but, the nugget we're after is, the things we didn't do well. We want to fashion a document of recommendations for improvement. This document can be used to amend our requirements, which in turn ultimately re-informs our design decisions.

This document, oftentimes, will consist of several observations. Following Chandler and Unger's *A Project Guide to UX Design* (2012), each observation will consist of, at least, three parts:

1. A short description to describe the context of the observation.
2. A perceived impact ranking ranging from low to high. Low impact rankings suggest the issue creates a minor problem but doesn't cause a noticeable break in the experience. Medium impact rankings suggest the issue causes the user some frustration, however, the issue is reversible. High impact rankings, like the well-laid plans of mice and men, suggest the issue directly causes the user to irreversibly fail the task they set out to accomplish.
3. Recommendations—These will be used to help focus efforts toward fixing the encountered problem.

As I'm not covering the entire list of heuristics in this book, I strongly recommend checking out Jakob Nielsen's: *10 Usability Heuristics for User Interface Design*; and Bruce "Tog" Tognazzini's: *First Principles of Interaction Design*. I use the former as an aperitif and the latter when I'm feeling a little risqué. Seriously, Tog's list is ridiculously detailed but over time, and with each new project, it becomes less intimidating.

THE RAINBOW STACK

Below are a few usability heuristics from Jakob Nielsen, which I always include in my projects:

- *Recognition rather than recall*—Minimize the user's memory load by making objects, actions, and options visible. The user should not have to remember information from one part of the dialogue to another. Instructions for using the system should be visible or easily retrievable whenever appropriate.
- *Aesthetic and minimalist design*—Dialogues should not contain information which is irrelevant or rarely needed. Every extra unit of information in a dialogue competes with the relevant units of information and diminishes their relative visibility. (Nielsen, 1994)

This being said, heuristic analysis does not replace user testing as there is a sizeable difference between *building the product right* and *building the right product*.

SURFACE

"Rules of taste enforce structures of power."

—Susan Sontag

We've finally arrived at our destination. The *Surface* plane is the tip of the product iceberg. It deals with the parts of our final product that our ship of users will be sure to notice. Continuing with our analogy, seeing that the Skeleton plane has been described as the muscle of our product, then it's only fitting that the Surface plane be described as the skin. It is the wrapping that holds everything together. While superficially this section may seem like a walk in the park, the Surface plane is not about adding different flavors to our wireframe pot. It facilitates a secret job and functions as an integral piece to the UX puzzle.

The goal is to use all the frills available, in our arsenal, to continually direct users' attention to important parts throughout the interface. The trick here is to achieve this *direction-ing* without the user becoming aware of our scheming ways. We'll know if our subconscious coercion worked when after a successful usability test, users' remark: "It was easy to use" or describe the product as intuitive. This is the brilliance of the

Surface plane; it has the power to create or break our carefully crafted user experience.

When thinking about the Surface plane, we should think of *Contrast*, *Color*, and *Typography*. User psychology also plays an important role here, as understanding how a user might react to a design choice can ultimately affect the success of the final product.

First is *Contrast*. It is one of the primary factors affecting the ease of *skim-ability* of the screen. It shouldn't be described in terms of black and white but rather, in terms of clarity and readability. Clarity is the promotion of the known over the novel. Ignoring convention for the sake of the shock factor may work in some professions; but, this isn't one of them. I'm speaking to you—the one who thinks it would be cool to place the menu icon on the bottom right corner of the screen. Readability, on the other hand, is the ease with which the user can read all the relevant text on the screen. A low readability level, in some cases, can often be a reason that users describe a product as difficult to use.

Next is *Color*. It has a wide range of uses; from the ability to convey meaning to eliciting desired user responses. Bold colors can be used to draw the user's attention to key elements within the prototype such as a call-to-action button. Specific colors can be used to effectively communicate a brand identity to the user. This is especially true for companies that use them consistently over the years—think Facebook's blue or Coca-Cola's red. Color can even be used to enhance readability by supporting contrast. How is this possible, you might be wondering? Well, have you ever tried to read *red* 12-point text on a *blue* background? You'll discover, just like a crocodile at an alligator convention, it's not a good fit. Color breathes life

THE RAINBOW STACK

into our prototype and as such, I like to think of it as the soul of the product.

Last is *Typography*. The standard definition of typography is the technique of arranging type to make written language legible and appealing when displayed. The purpose of type is communication. According to John Kane, in his work *A Type Primer*, if we *see* the type before we can discern the words, then it's time to change the type (Kane, 2002). In my opinion, type should convey within its form, a quality consistent with our product's message. After all, nothing screams "gain dominion over your music" like a script typeface. If you missed the sarcasm, please take note. Fortunately, with the advent of platform-specific type recommendations, using type has become markedly easier. For example, if tasked with designing for mobile phones, Google's Material Design: The Type System[4] and Apple's Human Interface Guidelines: Typography[5], are solid resources to check out. If, on the other hand, designing for the web, search for "type scale sites" on your search engine of choice, for similar results.

User psychology isn't just relegated to the Surface plane; it should be in the fore of our mind as we step onto the design train. For those astute readers that might be wondering: Why then is it only being discussed now? The answer is because it fits perfectly with the theme of the Surface plane. Understanding user psychology (*direction-ing* behind the scenes) will make the product more effective in its task of creating a seamless solution for our users' problems. We also want our product to be given a fair chance at reaching our users, and standing out, even in a sea of competition. Put another way, it doesn't matter how much time we spend designing the final product, or how well it meets our user needs, if we can't keep our users engaged long enough to find out.

Susan Weinschenk, in her book *100 Things Every Designer Needs to Know about People*, goes into a myriad of theories, concepts, and research studies on the topic. It's an easy read and I highly recommend it to anyone trying to get a jump on these sneaky user behaviors. Dr. Weinschenk drives home the point that as users, we all share one similar trait: the human condition. As such, though we may experience the world differently, the principles that govern our behavior remain the same. How we see, read, remember, think, feel, and ultimately decide to buy, can be codified and indulged.

Though *The Rainbow Stack* doesn't discuss user psychology in detail, I will go over a few of my favorite takeaways as they pertain to our streaming service app.

> *"Design with forgetting in mind. If some information is really important, don't rely on people to remember it. Provide it for them in your design, or have a way for them to easily look it up."* (Weinschenk, 2010)

As designers, there are limits to our power. We can't possibly anticipate every external condition our users may face while using our platform. It's fair to assume, however, that in some of these cases, our users' attention will become compromised. Whatever the reason, the user should never have to struggle to complete an in-app task; previously explained or otherwise.

> *"Don't expect that people will necessarily pay attention to information you provide."* (Weinschenk, 2010)

THE RAINBOW STACK

This is why directing their behaviors through the use of colors, typography, layout, and navigation is an invaluable asset. If ever we find ourselves questioning why some users—even after fashioning them with easy-to-follow instructions—are still so terribly lost, just remember: humans are going to *human*.

TEST

"If you cannot fail you cannot learn"

—Erick Ries

We've now come full circle. We started from a fledgling hypothesis; extracting our user needs, growing solutions through idea-generating maneuvers, and building wireframes from our requirements. Now we're a mature prototype. It's been quite the ride but we're not yet at the finish line. The final question we should ask ourselves is: Where do we go from here?

If you recall, during our initial round of interviews, we only implemented Acts I and II of Jake Knapp's "Five-Act Interview" process. We did this, not because there's a problem with Knapp's methodology, but because we didn't have a prototype for our users to test. So, that's what we'll be doing in this last section of *The Rainbow Stack*. Dust the cobwebs off your white coat and grab your clipboard because we will now revisit the test lands.

This time around, instead of trying to obtain a rich set of data to use to create user personas, we're interested in our user's ability to successfully complete key actions within our product. This is called the *usability test*. Its purpose according to NN/g, is to identify problems in the design of the product, uncover opportunities to improve, and learn about our target user's preferences (Moran, 2019).

As we continue to the good stuff, we will have to restart the interview process. During Act I, the friendly introduction, we start with an easygoing but structured conversation. Remember we're trying to put the previous interviewees (participants) at ease. During Act II, we ask a series of open-ended context questions about the participant. We do this; one: because we genuinely care about the people we interview and two: it helps reopen the participant's worldview.

During Act III, we introduce the prototype to our participants. Since we don't know if our interpretation of our users' needs has adequately addressed their problem, no development work should be started as of yet. In its stead, we'll use a rapid prototype, of the Surface plane variety. Rapid prototyping is a quick and cost-effective way to test a functioning version of our product. This works by creating a network of static screens linked via *hotspots*, which give the impression of interactivity. According to Knapp (2016), at this point, we should reinforce the status of the relationship by asking the participant if they'd be willing to look at some prototypes. Once they begin, oftentimes, they forget that they aren't actually using a live product. It's also important to tell the participant that there are no wrong answers and that we didn't design the prototype. Yes, we're lying but it's for a good cause. You see, false-positives are still an ever-looming threat to our success. It's much easier for participants to be honest if they don't believe we're emotionally attached to the presented ideas.

During Act IV, we give the participant a light nudge so they react to the prototype. The goal is to observe their behavior. I usually call this act: the freedom of movement stage. It's one of the easiest to get right but it's also one of the easiest to get wrong. The rules are simple, the participant must:

1. Think aloud
2. Truthfully answer every open-ended question we ask
3. Be given full autonomy over their journey

The last rule is probably the most important as no one likes to be told what to do. Furthermore, telling participants what to do is a waste of a moderated usability test and we may as well save ourselves the effort and run a remote, unmoderated test. So, how do we start this *nudge*; well the proof is in the pudding. Knapp suggests beginning with a simple: "How would you do X?" then follow-up with a series of questions to aid in the first rule.

- What might this be for?
- What do you think about that?
- What's going through your mind as you see this?
- What would you do next? (Knapp et al., 2016)

During the final act, Act V, we ask a few debriefing questions to recapture the participant's main thoughts about the experience. All things considered, we could sift through all the data received thus far and pick out the pertinent bits ourselves. But isn't it better when people do the hard work for us? Call it lazy or whatever; I call it good ole fashioned efficiency. To help jog our participant's memory, we'll ask a few specific questions.

- How does this product compare to what you do now?
- What did you like about this product?
- What did you dislike?
- How would you describe this product to a friend? (Knapp et al., 2016)

Last, we thank the participant for their time and ask if there's anything else they'd like to add. With this, we conclude our usability tests. Be prepared for plot twists and user reveals, as things seldom ever go exactly as planned. If any design problems are uncovered, we'll have to iterate over this process once again. Think of it as having to respawn at whichever checkpoint the problem arose. We also have to be very thorough with our approach in order to mitigate the chance of a possible Groundhog Day event; where we'll be stuck in an iterative loop.

This brings us to the end of *The Rainbow Stack*'s "Build" process. I know it was a bit work intensive, with a lot of theory and not many examples, but hey who said this was going to be easy? Just remember that as rough as this may seem, it's still leagues above the nearest alternative, that is, building your dream product—that fits no real need, trying to minimize your inevitable churn and burn while waiting on customers to see your *obvious* value.

Before continuing to the conclusion, it's useful to run through a visual summary of what we've learned throughout this section.

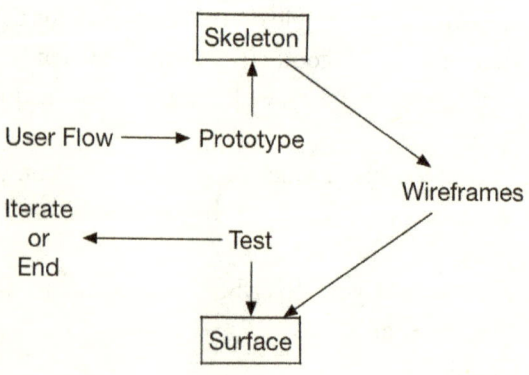

THE RAINBOW STACK

- We started with the user or task flow produced by our idea factory—it was the fuel for our prototype fire.
- Next, was the prototype stage, which houses the Skeleton and Surface planes—these can be thought of as the facilitator of the try-before-you-buy approach.
- The Skeleton plane is like the muscular system—it's built on top of the user flows and focuses on creating design components of varying levels of detail.
- The agent of the Skeletal plane is the wireframe—it is arguably the most recognizable tool of the UX process and conveys our design's form.
- The Surface plane has a secret job of directing the user's attention to important parts of the design throughout the interface.
- Last, was the test stage—it probes the user's ability to complete key actions within our product.
- After the testing, we either end or iterate.

Notes

[4] https://material.io/design/typography/the-type-system.html
[5] https://developer.apple.com/design/human-interface-guidelines/ios/visual-design/typography/

CONCLUSION

"A true thing, poorly expressed, is a lie."

—Stephen Fry

So, we've now reached the end of the rainbow—the magical place where we go to fulfill our dreams. Sorry, there are no leprechauns but, as promised, let's get your pot of gold. Though I could share the golden lump sum in its entirety, I think it's best to take more of an annuity-based approach. You might be wondering: Why should we have to wait? I mean, after all, we've made it through the entire book. Well, as you'll soon see, the answer centers around complexity.

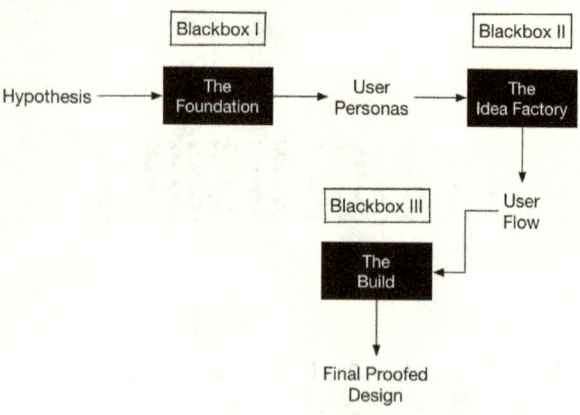

If we look at the UX design process in terms of a series of black box systems, it simplifies the final roadmap enormously. The arrows going into the boxes represent inputs while the arrows emerging from the boxes are outputs. Outputs from one system are used as inputs to a subsequent one; until the final proofed design is achieved.

Why does the above process seem so simple? Well, that's sort of the point. In the above diagram, a greater emphasis was placed on what each section of *The Rainbow Stack* produced, rather than how it functioned. But what goes into the black box? We can replace the black boxes with their visual summaries—the diagrams found at the end of each section.

With this out of the way, we can finally move on to the moment we've all been waiting for; the unabridged roadmap of the complete user experience puzzle. If at first glance, it seems like you're being inundated with a lot of information, that's probably because you are. Due to the sheer size of the full roadmap, it's split into three manageable morsels. Once the morsels are properly digested, we'll then fit them all together to reveal the big picture.

THE RAINBOW STACK

Drum rolls, please …

To make sense of the illustrations below, it's important to keep a few things in mind. The broader of the two arrow strokes represents directionality, or flow, whereas the thinner arrow stroke, represents the UX techniques of which the component consists. I'll try to use these illustrative morsels to briefly cover key takeaways, as well as, any concepts which I chose to omit during the process.

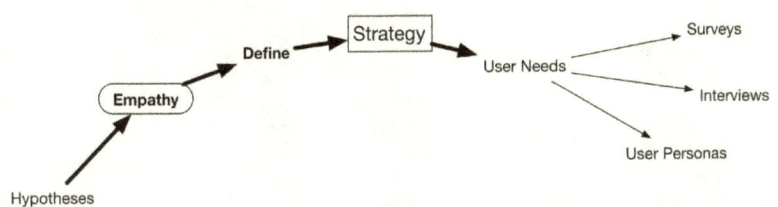

The first piece of the puzzle shows Black Box Number 1: *The Foundation*. Please note that it's impossible to create our prized user personas without first conducting our user interviews. The takeaway here is that there are no shortcuts during the laying of our foundation.

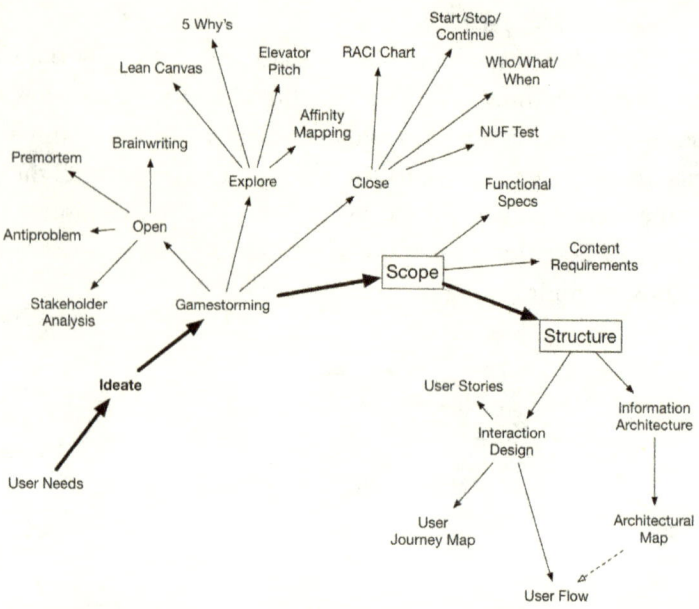

The second piece of the puzzle describes Black Box Number 2: *The Idea Factory*. Yes, it's quite involved, so I'll take it slow. We'll start with the Scope plane, which is broken into two parts: functional specifications and content requirements. Unlike functional specs, content requirements aren't directly informed by our user needs. They can, however, be handed down to us by the project stakeholders. Next, to round out this morsel, we continue with the Structure plane. The one thing I didn't discuss here is the user story. User stories help summarize the user's desires from their point of view. These take the following form: As a [user] I want [feature] so that I can [insert a need]. I usually cut a few corners at this point and glean this information directly from the user persona and affinity maps. This is not to say they aren't important, I just tend not to use them. These can be a useful guide when moving toward the user journey map.

THE RAINBOW STACK

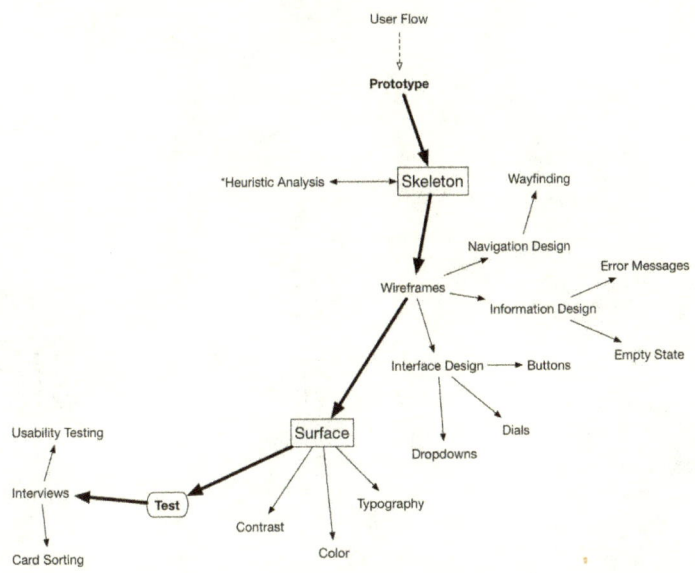

The final piece of the puzzle describes Black Box Number 3: *The Build*. Everything is this morsel has pretty much been covered, except for card sorting. Card sorting is an activity, which is carried out during the Testing stage, where participants are given items printed on cards. Their task is to place these items into groups that make sense. When is this used? If our user gets stuck at some point within the prototype, and our iterative approach yields little results, a card sort may be a viable solution. We can kick things off by asking the participants to place the cards into pre-made categories; this is known as a *closed sort*. Or, we could ask them to create their own categories while sorting; this is called an *open sort*. Now that we've covered the various pieces of the user experience puzzle, let's take a look at the resulting roadmap.

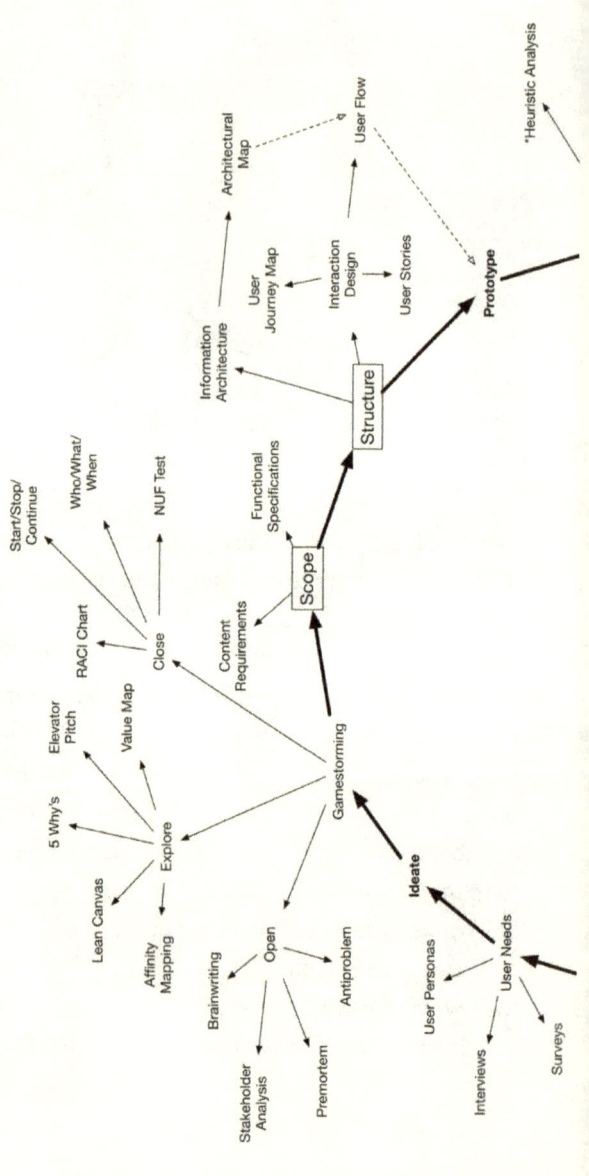

THE RAINBOW STACK

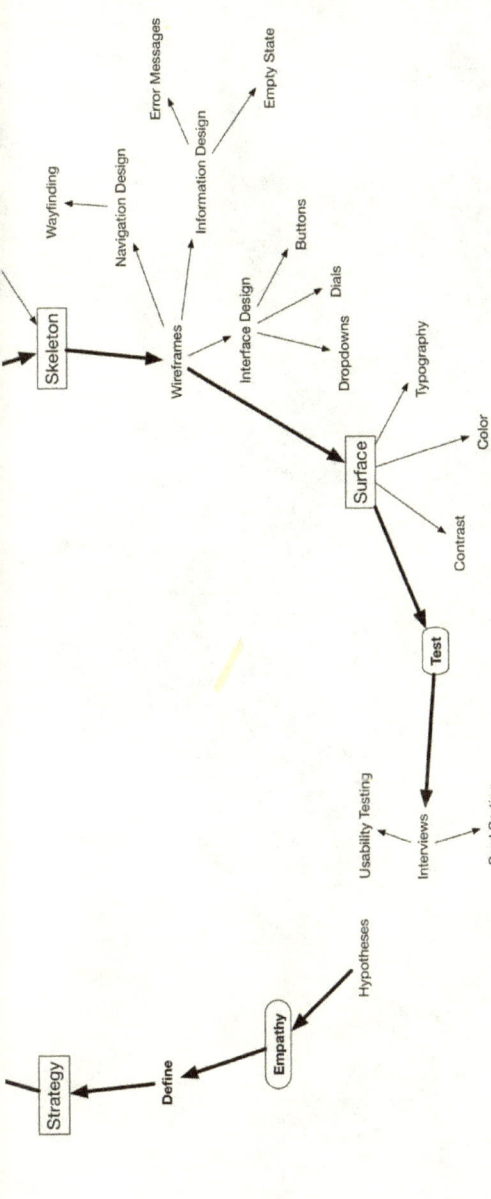

And it's a wrap. Isn't she beautiful? Well, I hope the payoff was worth the read. In the event that it wasn't, just remember: it's the journey that counts, not the final destination. Unless of course, crossing the finish line earns us a few million dollars. In that case, final destination away.

BIBLIOGRAPHY

Garrett, Jesse James. *Elements of user experience, the: user-centered design for the web and beyond.* Pearson Education, 2010.

Gibbons, S. (2018, December 9th). *Journey Mapping 101.* Nielsen Norman Group. https://www.nngroup.com/articles/journey-mapping-101/

Gray, Dave, Sunni Brown, and James Macanufo. *Gamestorming: A playbook for innovators, rulebreakers, and changemakers.* "O'Reilly Media, Inc.", 2010.

Hall, Erika. *Just enough research.* New York: A Book Apart, 2013.

Kane, John. *A type primer.* Laurence King Publishing, 2002.

Knapp, Jake, John Zeratsky, and Braden Kowitz. *Sprint: How to solve big problems and test new ideas in just five days.* Simon and Schuster, 2016.

Maurya, Ash. *Running lean: iterate from plan A to a plan that works.* "O'Reilly Media, Inc.", 2012.

Moore, Geoffrey A., and Regis McKenna. "Crossing the chasm". (1999).

Moran, Kate. (2019, December 9th). Usability Testing 101. Nielsen Norman Group. https://www.nngroup.com/articles/usability-testing-101/

Nielsen, Jakob. (1994, April 24th). 10 Usability Heuristics for User Interface Design. Nielsen Norman Group. https://www.nngroup.com/articles/ten-usability-heuristics/

Norman, Don. *The design of everyday things: Revised and expanded edition.* Basic books, 2013

Ries, Eric. *The lean startup: How today's entrepreneurs use continuous innovation to create radically successful businesses.* Currency, 2011.

Rosenfeld, Louis, Peter Morville, and Jorge Arango. *Information Architecture: For the Web and Beyond.* "O'Reilly Media, Inc.", 2015.

Unger, Russ, and Carolyn Chandler. *A Project Guide to UX Design: For user experience designers in the field or in the making.* New Riders, 2012.

Waloszek, Gerd. (2012, September 12th). Introduction to Design Thinking. SAP User Experience Community. https://experience.sap.com/skillup/introduction-to-design-thinking/

Weinschenk, Susan. *100 things every designer needs to know about people.* Pearson Education, 2011.

CPSIA information can be obtained
at www.ICGtesting.com
Printed in the USA
LVHW042345030423
743403LV00006B/747